Cluck Cluck

S0-ADW-621

Potholders

and Other Loopy Projects

by Barbara Kane

KLUTZ

Weaving 101

Over, Under, Around and Through

You are about to become one of a long line (some say it goes 8,000 years back) of human beings who have woven a useful or beautiful piece of fabric from a jumbled pile of thread or yarn.

Like most of those before you, you will do this using a simple tool, a hand loom. Your own fingers will do the rest.

your pile of loops

your hand loom

Worthwhile Weaving Words

To learn to weave, it helps to know two words:

WARP — The loops (or yarn) stretched on the loom before weaving

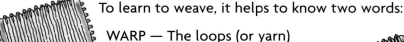

warp loops

WEFT — The loops woven over and under the warp loops.

weft loop

warp loops

Weaving Workshop

1 Pick out colors for your first square – 18 warp loops to stretch on the loom, and 18 weft loops to weave over and under the warp.

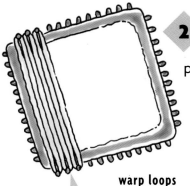

2 Stretch the warp loops across the loom. Put one loop on every pair of pegs.

warp loops

TIP:
If you run out of pegs on one side, but not the other, you've skipped a peg somewhere. Find the place and adjust the loops.

3

3 Take your first weft loop and begin to weave it over and under the warp loops. Go OVER both strands of the first warp loop and UNDER both strands of the second loop.

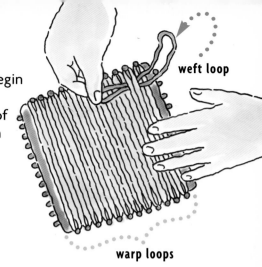

weft loop

warp loops

weft loop

warp loops

4 Keep weaving the weft loop over or under each warp loop.

5 Pull the front end of the loop toward the far side of the loom, and catch the tail end on the peg.

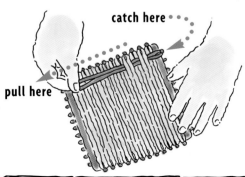

catch here

pull here

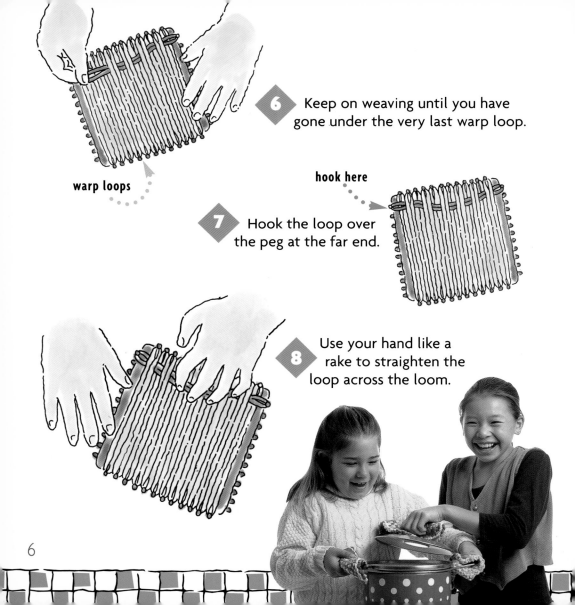

6 Keep on weaving until you have gone under the very last warp loop.

warp loops

hook here

7 Hook the loop over the peg at the far end.

8 Use your hand like a rake to straighten the loop across the loom.

second weft loop

go UNDER not OVER this loop

9 IMPORTANT: Start to weave in the second weft loop differently from the first. Go UNDER the first warp loop this time, OVER the second warp loop, and so on.

weft loops

10 Continue weaving the rest of the weft loops. Remember to switch back and forth as you begin each row: Go OVER the first warp loop in row one, UNDER the first loop in the next row.

warp loops

11 Every row or two, use your hands as rakes to straighten the weaving.

12 If the last few loops are hard to weave, use your crochet hook to catch and pull them through.

crochet hook

Leave your potholder on the loom until you finish the edges. Use woven edging (page 10) or loopy edging (page 26).

Once the edges are finished, you've got yourself a potholder. Keep it handy for all your potholding needs or, better yet, give it as a gift. Many cooks think woven potholders are the best kind around, but they can't buy them in stores — they have to know someone with a loom who will weave some for them.

If you want a greater challenge, flip through the book and pick a non-potholder project.

WARP loops go in first, then WEFT (it's alphabetical)!

Woven Edging

This is the easiest way to finish off a potholder.

You will need:
◆ **A square that you've finished weaving, still on the loom**
◆ **A crochet hook**

loop 1

1 Holding the loom so that one corner is pointing away from you, find the top loop on the right-hand side. This is loop 1.

crochet hook

loop 1

loop 2

2 Catch loop 1 with your crochet hook and pull it off its peg.

loop 2

loop 1

3 With loop 1 still on the crochet hook, poke the hook through the top loop on the left-hand side of the loom, and pull it off its peg. This is loop 2

4 Lift **loop 1** with your fingers and pull **loop 2** through it using the hook to grab and pull it through. Now you have only one loop on your hook again – **loop 2**.

5 With that loop still on the hook, poke the hook through the next loop to the left, and pull it off its peg. This is **loop 3**.

6 Repeat step 4, lifting **loop 2** with your fingers, and pulling **loop 3** through it using the hook. Once again you have only one loop on your hook.

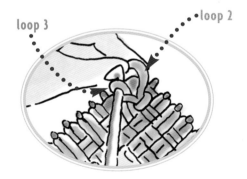

11

6 Keep going along like this, always moving to the left. Be careful to keep the loops ahead of you on their pegs! When you come to a corner, just weave right around it, no need to change your technique.

work in this direction

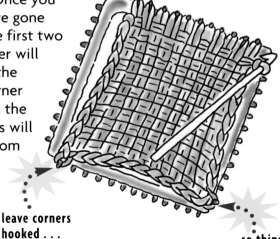

7 Once you have gone around the first two sides, one corner will be completely loose from the loom. Stretch the loose corner back and catch a loop from the edging on a corner peg. This will keep the weaving on the loom until you finish the edging.

Catch the next corner, too, once it's free.

leave corners hooked . . .

. . . so things stay organized

pull the last loop out extra far

8 Keep weaving the edge all the way around the square until you come to the very last loop. Pull this loop through extra far, so it won't pop back out.

9 Take your potholder off the loom and pull it this way and that to work it back into a square shape. That's it! A finished potholder that can be machine washed and dried.

Done!

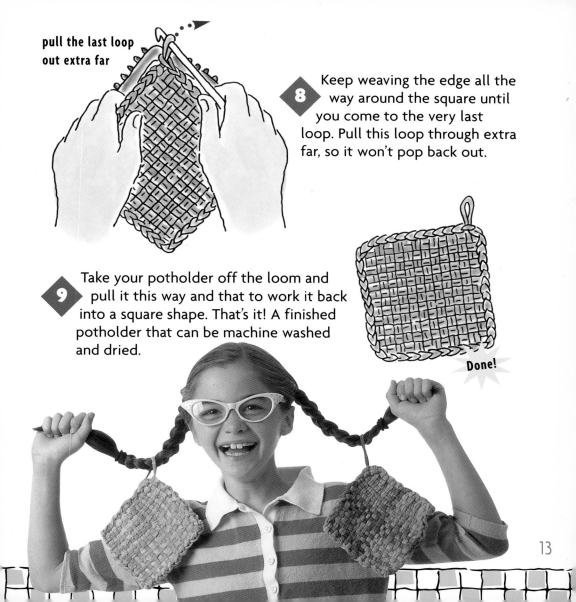

Turn a potholder into a
Picture Frame

You will need:
- ◆ **A potholder**
- ◆ **A photo**
- ◆ **2 slender twigs, 5 ½ inches long**
- ◆ **Yarn, 15 inches long**
- ◆ **Crochet hook**

1 Center your photo on the potholder and lay the twigs over it as shown.

2 Find the four loops in the weaving that are right beneath the twigs and beside the photo. The red arrows are pointing to them.

3 Use your crochet hook to pull the four loops up and stretch them.

crochet hook

4 Slip the twigs through the stretched loops.

5 Tie a piece of yarn to the top corners to make a picture hanger and slip the photo into its place behind the twigs.

Weaving Patterns

By arranging your warp and weft loops in a particular order, you can create a pattern as you weave. Just weave over and under as usual.

1 Follow this part of the pattern to arrange your warp loops on the loom. Each little oval in this row shows the color for one warp loop.

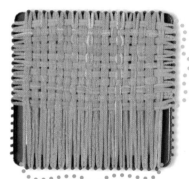

weft loops

warp loops

2 Then weave the weft loops in the order shown here. Each oval in this row shows the color for one weft loop.

Stripes
2 COLORS

This one's super easy — just alternate between pink and green loops.

You can use your choice of colors in any of the patterns.

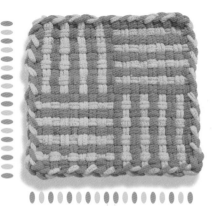

2

2

Colors alternate except for the two in the middle.

Pinwheel

2 COLORS

Just one tiny difference changes the Stripes pattern on page 16 into the Pinwheel pattern!

weft loop colors

Puzzle Pieces

2 COLORS

This potholder is made by using three of the first color, then three of the second color, then back to three of the first color again, and so on.

warp loop colors

Woven Purse

You will need:

- ◆ **2 potholders finished with woven edges (page 10)**
- ◆ **1 yard yarn**
- ◆ **Plastic needle**
- ◆ **10–14 extra loops for the strap**

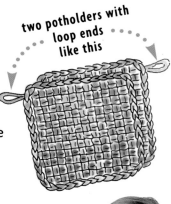

two potholders with loop ends like this

How to make the Bag

1 Lay one square on top of the other with the end loops placed as shown.

2 Tie one end of the yarn at the base of one of the end loops. Thread the needle with the other end.

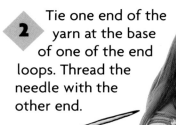

3 Beginning at the base of the loop, sew the squares together. Poke the needle through both squares, pull it through, and then start another stitch right next to the spot where the needle first went in.

4 Sew down one side, across the bottom, and up the other side to the other end loop. Leave the top open.

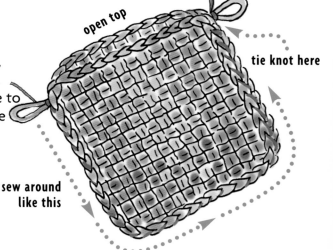

open top

tie knot here

sew around like this

Remove the needle and tie the yarn at the base of the loop.

How to make the Strap

end loop · ·

5 Put a loop through one of the end loops on the purse, taking one end of the loop with each hand.

6 Pass the loop ends from hand-to-hand four or five times. Always pass the loop you find in your right hand through the loop you find in your left hand.

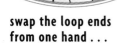

swap the loop ends from one hand . . .

. . . to the other, 4 or 5 times

21

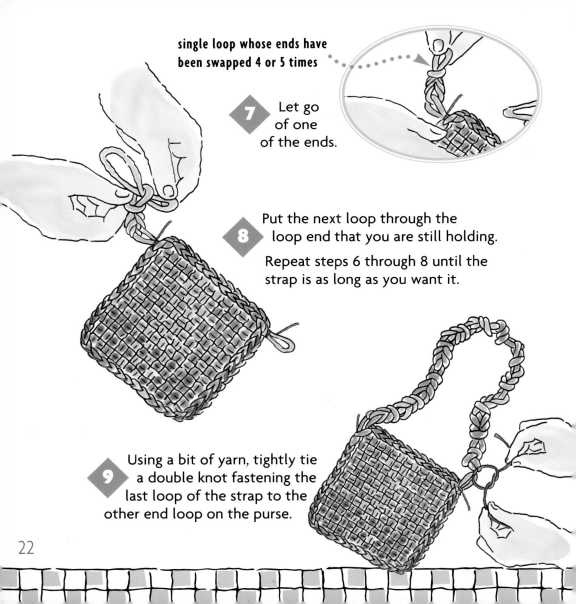

single loop whose ends have
been swapped 4 or 5 times

7 Let go
of one
of the ends.

8 Put the next loop through the
loop end that you are still holding.

Repeat steps 6 through 8 until the
strap is as long as you want it.

9 Using a bit of yarn, tightly tie
a double knot fastening the
last loop of the strap to the
other end loop on the purse.

Purse Patterns

Sky-Blue Purse

5 COLORS

Remember! WARP loops first, then WEFT

warp colors

Rainbow Purse

4 COLORS
For the purse shown on page 20.

6 loops of one color

6 loops of another

6 loops of the first

6 loops of one color   6 of a second   6 of the first color

23

Make MINI Game-Boards

t i c
t a c
t o e

2 COLORS
Weave as usual.

5

2

2

weft colors

warp colors

5

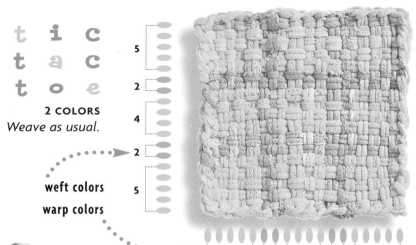

5   2   4   2   5

16

16

Checkers

3 COLORS

To get the checkerboard pattern, weave the red loops, two at a time, over and under pairs of the blue loops.

You can use buttons or coins
as playing pieces — 6 for each player
in tic tac toe, and 12 for each player in checkers.

Loopy edging

This is the second way to finish a potholder. The first is woven edging (page 10). If you're making a project that needs two squares woven together, this is the edging you'll have to have.

You will need:

- ◆ **A woven square, still on the loom**
- ◆ **2 ½ yards of yarn**
- ◆ **A crochet hook**

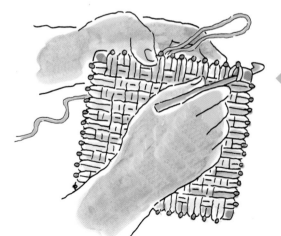

1 Fold one end of the yarn over 3-4 inches to make a loop.

2 Hold the loom up on edge on the table, and use the crochet hook to reach through the far right loop on the top edge of the loom.

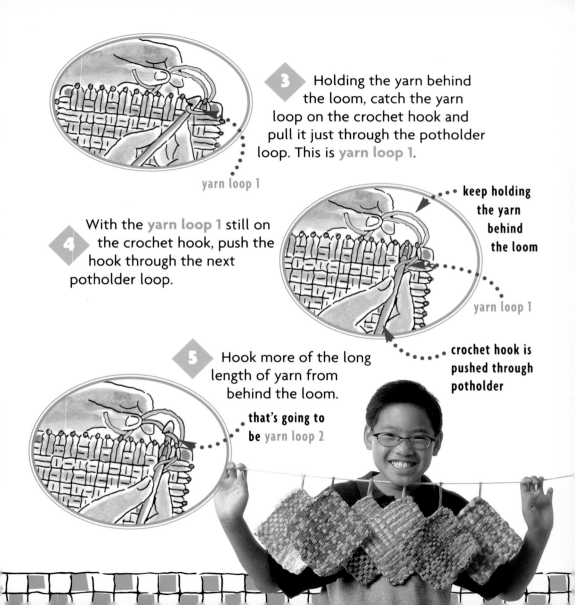

3 Holding the yarn behind the loom, catch the yarn loop on the crochet hook and pull it just through the potholder loop. This is **yarn loop 1**.

yarn loop 1

4 With the **yarn loop 1** still on the crochet hook, push the hook through the next potholder loop.

keep holding the yarn behind the loom

yarn loop 1

crochet hook is pushed through potholder

5 Hook more of the long length of yarn from behind the loom.

that's going to be **yarn loop 2**

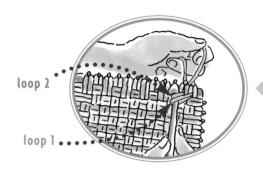

loop 2

loop 1

6 Pull **yarn loop 2** back through the potholder loop.

7 Twist the crochet hook to face away from you, and wiggle **yarn loop 2** through **yarn loop 1**, letting **yarn loop 1** slip off the crochet hook. You will again have just one yarn loop on your crochet hook.

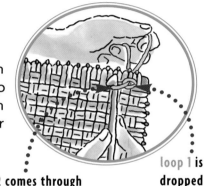

loop 2 comes through

loop 1 is dropped

8 Repeat steps 4 through 7. After a few more yarn loops, let go of the short end of the yarn. Keep holding the long yarn from behind the loom as you continue around the square.

cut here · · · · ·

9 When you come back to the first potholder loop, pull a yarn loop through it in the usual way, but keep pulling until it's 2 to 3 inches long. Cut the yarn near the hook.

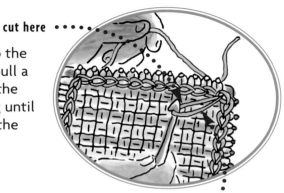

loop is 2 or 3 inches long

backside view

10 Use the crochet hook, coming from behind the loom, to pull the remaining end of the yarn through to the back. Tie the two loose ends in a double knot and trim them to ¼ inch. Done!

Big Bean Bag

You will need:
- ◆ **2 potholders finished with loopy edges**
- ◆ **Crochet hook**
- ◆ **1 pound dry lima or kidney beans**

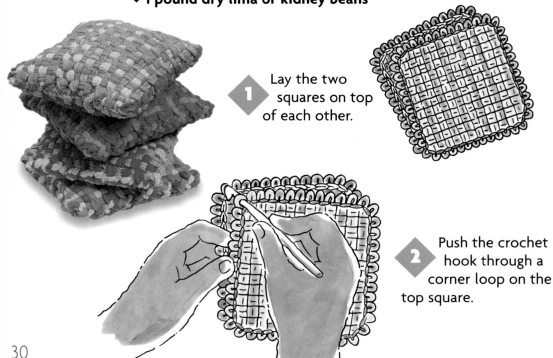

1 Lay the two squares on top of each other.

2 Push the crochet hook through a corner loop on the top square.

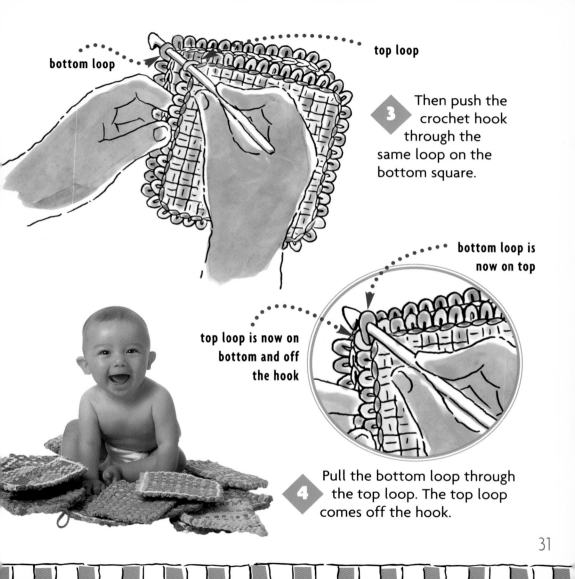

bottom loop

top loop

3 Then push the crochet hook through the same loop on the bottom square.

bottom loop is now on top

top loop is now on bottom and off the hook

4 Pull the bottom loop through the top loop. The top loop comes off the hook.

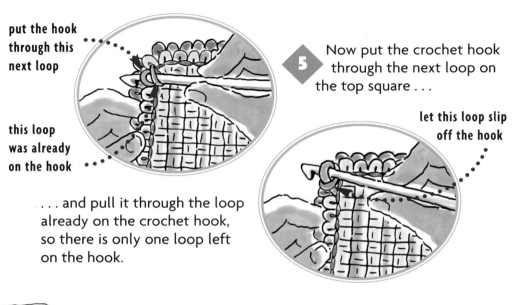

put the hook through this next loop

this loop was already on the hook

5 Now put the crochet hook through the next loop on the top square . . .

let this loop slip off the hook

. . . and pull it through the loop already on the crochet hook, so there is only one loop left on the hook.

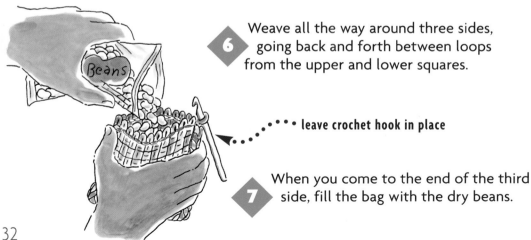

Beans

6 Weave all the way around three sides, going back and forth between loops from the upper and lower squares.

leave crochet hook in place

7 When you come to the end of the third side, fill the bag with the dry beans.

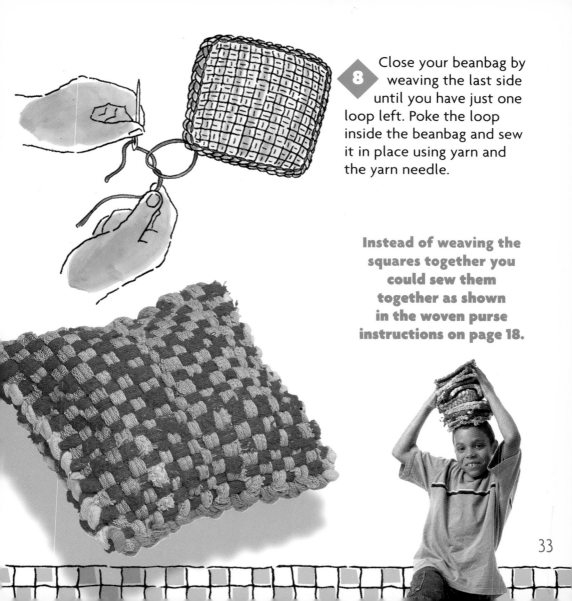

8 Close your beanbag by weaving the last side until you have just one loop left. Poke the loop inside the beanbag and sew it in place using yarn and the yarn needle.

Instead of weaving the squares together you could sew them together as shown in the woven purse instructions on page 18.

More Weaving

Classic

This pattern goes like this: nine loops of one color . . .

. . . followed by nine loops of a second color.

9

9

9   9

Fiesta

6 COLORS

six of one color

six of a second color

six of a third color

six of a fourth color

six of a fifth color

six of a sixth color

34

Patterns

Hound's Tooth

2 COLORS

Two loops of one color followed by two loops of a second color, etc.

weft colors

warp colors

weft colors are all one color

Confetti

5 COLORS

five warp colors take turns

Loopy Chicken

You will need:

- ◆ **1 potholder with loopy edges**
- ◆ **8 cotton balls**
- ◆ **8 yellow loops**
- ◆ **Yarn — 15 inches red and 15 inches blue**
- ◆ **Crochet hook and plastic needle**

Body

1 Stuff potholders with cotton balls and fold as shown.

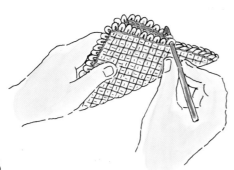

2 Starting at one end, weave the edges together as shown in the Big Bean Bag instructions on page 30.

Comb, Wattle & Eye

Use the multi-colored yarn to sew on these features.

comb

wattle

Check out my lovely Comb and Wattle.

3 Thread the needle with 15 inches of red yarn. Make a knot at the end that is the most reddish.

15 inches long

4 Sew loopy stitches to make the comb and wattle as shown.

Start with a small tight stitch, then make a long loopy stitch that you leave loose. Next make another small tight stitch. Go back and forth between loopy and tight stitches and make a knot at the end.

loose stitch

tight stitch

5 Thread the needle with blue yarn and make a knot at one end.

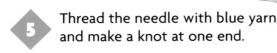

knot

6 Sew a few stitches on each side of the head to make the eyes. Make a knot when finished.

Tail feathers

7 Use your crochet hook to pull each yellow loop halfway through a loop in the weaving as shown. Play around with the tail until you like the way it looks.

To See the

full line of 100% Klutz certified products, fill in this postcard, pop on a stamp, drop it in the mail and wait impatiently for our mail order catalog to arrive. Or check us out at our web site.

KLUTZ.com
Come on in!

OPEN 24 HOURS

Klutz Catalog!

You can order the entire library of 100% Klutz certified books, more loops, and a diverse collection of other things we happen to like from The Klutz Catalog. It is, in all modesty, unlike any other catalog — and it's yours for the asking.

Who are you?

Name: _____ Age: _____ ☐ Too high to count ○ Boy ○ Girl

Address: _____

City: _____ State: _____ Zip: _____

My Bright Ideas!

Tell us what you think of this book: _____

What would you like us to write a book about? _____

☐ Check this box if you want us to send you The Klutz Catalog.

If you're a grown-up who'd like to hear about new Klutz stuff, give us your e-mail address and we'll stay in touch.

E-mail address: _____

Potholders

More Great Books from Klutz

Origami

Window Art

Painted Rocks

The Shrinky Dinks® Book

Making Mini-Books

KLUTZ
455 Portage Avenue
Palo Alto, CA 94306

PLACE
FIRST
CLASS
POSTAGE
HERE